CLEAR EYE TEA

Mary Bonina

Červená Barva Press
Somerville, Massachusetts

Červená Barva Press
P.O. Box 440357
W. Somerville, MA 02144-3222

www.cervenabarvapress.com

Bookstore: www.thelostbookshelf.com

Cover Photograph: Mary Bonina
"Herring Cove, Campobello Island, N.B."

Author Photograph: Unknown, author's personal archive

Cover Design: William J. Kelle

Production: Jennifer LeBlanc

ISBN: 978-0-9844732-9-8

Library of Congress: 2010936910

ACKNOWLEDGEMENTS

I am grateful to all those who listened to these poems while they were in progress, including the friends and editors of Hanging Loose Press, Members of the Writers Room of Boston, supporters of the Červená Barva Press reading series, the New England Poetry Club, Will Delman and the Bay State Underground crowd at Boston University, Tapestry of Voices, Chapter and Verse, and the Brookline Public Library poetry group. Thanks to Mark Pawlak, Dick Lourie, Frannie Lindsay, John Dufresne and Edward P. Jones who commented on these poems or otherwise offered support and inspiration; and to other members of my posse: Joan Eisenberg, Paul Horan, Jackie Lawn, John Corcoran, Nancy Sawyer and Rachel Walker whose unflagging encouragement has helped me sustain faith in my work. Thanks to Abbi Sauro, William J. Kelle, and Andrai Whitted for technical help. I am indebted to the Virginia Center for the Creative Arts and the Writers Room of Boston, Inc. for providing exceptional working conditions during the writing of these poems. And I want to express great gratitude to Gloria Mindock, the editor/publisher of Červená Barva Press, who pushed me to get my work to see the light of day and worked hard to make it happen. Special thanks to Fred Marchant, Dzvinia Orlowsky, and John Skoyles for their willingness to read and comment on the manuscript.

These poems were originally published in the following journals and magazines: *Salamander*: "Sheep Shack" and (forthcoming) "All Souls;" *Hanging Loose*: "Selling Her Car." *Istanbul Literary Review*: "Sunday Drive to Visit Mum," "I Bring," "Dressing Room," "Receiving Guests," and "Doubt."

Living Proof, a chapbook (Červená Barva Press, 2007) included the poems "Shrine in Cambridge," "Lover Boy Fiction," and "Observing the Orchestra" (the latter formerly part of a longer poem called "Observing the Children's Orchestra").

An audio version of "Mountain Road from Roseau" is accessible on the author's website: http://www.marybonina.com.

TABLE OF CONTENTS

Four

Five

for Mark and Gianni

CLEAR EYE TEA

Clear Eye Tea

At the pier glass table
curative herbs dispensed,
the white-bearded man
with a scale looking
in the mirror over his head,
but not at me: he's heard
a jingle, the strap of bells shaken
where it's tied to the door knob,
someone coming in. But not

for deer tail, antler, shark fin,
not powder, oil, or capsule,
leaf, flower, or ground bone;
he's come to place a bet,
heading into the back room,
pushing aside the dark curtain.

The two things happening
make me think, don't we all
spend currency in the same shop?

In the vestibule of the gambling parlor,
standing at the great wall of tea,
sizing up shelves of tiny tins and boxes,
reading the offerings, appreciating
the promises illustrated
like pictures in children's books:

Hive Buster Tea and "that dieter's drink,"
Three Ballerina Tea, hoping
for a glow from *Complexion Tea,*
wondering if relief really will come
from *Muscle, Spine, and Back Tea;*

wanting most though the one
that helps with everything,
the one called *Clear Eye Tea.*

ONE

"The young know what you mean. The young are people
Tell them the difficulties can't be counted
and let them see not only what will be
but see with clarity these present times."

Yevgeny Yevtushenko

Compare and Contrast

When I put the photographs next to each other
they look the way ants do next to peonies,
together standing for more
than each would alone:
emitting both darkness and light,
color and its absence,
offering body and soul.

These two pictures lifted
from family albums, my inheritance:
mother and father in childhood worlds,
the one coddled, the other not.

In the sepia toned studio photograph,
my mother sitting and her sister
standing and holding onto her because
they have been living in separate houses
or if not yet, they will be soon,
the brother dying in his crib.
Is that the reason for the silk ribbon
threaded through cuffs of their baby socks,
tied in bows by their mother
who also sewed their perfect white frocks?

But the other photograph is dark, taken in a church —
First Holy Communion, my uncle thinks —
marble pillar so substantial behind the children
who look like waifs,
the tall girl, my father's oldest sister,
a six inch hem on her dress says hand-me-down
and my father himself with his arm protectively around
his little brother in short pants that once were long
and boot shoes on my father so scuffed up
and one eye already dead and no one knows it.

All Souls

"Parties don't change anything but they make us feel better."
from *La Pointe*, a film by Agnes Varda

It had been decided that
the day was not as holy
as the one before it

so who would imagine
anyone came to climb
the outside granite steps,

to press the center button
on the brass door knob, then enter
to climb the winding staircase,

to knock and sing *Surprise!*
No music in the house, not even
a doorbell. Was this a party?

Had there been snow falling —
always expected when wind
was stinging the oak leaves,

sissing them while chimes went on
in the neighbor's yard? What was wrong with
being angry at darkness descending too early,

everyone in not needing to be called
home, expecting something different,
what would properly meet the occasion?

There should have been cake
and candles and a song sung,
and there would have been:

if we had been able to think
of birth without also thinking
of death, if nerves carried
the right signals, if money
was not tight, if the boy wasn't sickly,
if wishes had been granted.

Eyes

The peacock's,
Evil's,
the storm's,
God's

and my father's.
I was his guide,
the one with good eyes.

I found the lost button, the earring,
saw the tiny spider floating
in the cup of wine at the picnic.

I captured a perfect photograph
without technical training,
found money in the gutter,
easily pushed a thin thread
through the needle opening.

I was blessed:
the family called me Hawkeye.

Diorama

Home in a shoebox world
I built an altar at which
I made my sisters pray.

Our Eucharist, the perfect candy
circles leaving Amen dust on the tongue.
I knew what was needed, what was missing.

Gather no flowers, but sprigs for our shrine,
some parsley cut from the yard to stand
like trees in thimbles of water.

We prepared to hold Mass
without a priest. We lived in a village
where we had no one to celebrate,

took matters into our own hands.
This was a new religion: we took a vow
we would give the nuns the third degree.

I liked it that my sweater
was buttoned all wrong.
I was a schoolgirl, always in a hurry.

The Reindeer of Green Hill

Bending to us, rubbing icy noses
against our small palms,
kissing up bread crusts and carrots.

We checked for which ones
had shed antlers, tried to read
watery brown eyes, worried
for a limp, a patch of skin worn off.

My father came forward
at the factory yard. He was
the favorite reindeer,
kissing us through chain links,

all four kids visiting at supper time,
crazy missing him, always working.

The whistle blew and my father
appeared with the herd of men
outside the loading dock.

We brought him sweets:
a cookie or a plum
pushed through the fence.

We collected his kisses.

Letters to the Virgin

When April got lost
in summer and evergreen
shades on the windows
had to be pulled,

rows of ceiling lights
switched off, I liked
the darkened classroom.

Clothed in lighter fabric
though kept in uniform,
pinned on our lapels

the miraculous medal, real gold,
threaded through baby blue
silk ribbons and worn all May:

we were stamped
with the Virgin's image.

Our sweaty little hands
moved across nicks, cheat notes
carved in ancient wooden desks
as we wrote letters to her

with *Lindy* blue ballpoint pens,
the only kind acceptable
for Palmer method handwriting,
slanted like a ladder propped
against the sky from hell to heaven.

We begged the Virgin,
mother of all,
take care of us,

intercede for the cousin
with the drug problem,
the friend's crippled brother,
father without a job, motherless child.

Anything and everything:
no censor, no human eye,
or so we were told, would ever read

our letters of supplication
going up in flames, burned
in the convent furnace,

smoke drifting straight up
to Our Lady who must
have been able to translate
the blackest soot,
discern meaning.

Bonfires

Back then what was customary,
we thought universal.

Take for example the bonfires,
the practice of putting out after dark
furniture and more than furniture,
taken through narrow hallways,
or dragged down several flights
to be torched in the street:

the sofa seeping horsehair,
the kitchen table with enamel top
("It won't burn!), the end table,
wooden pole lamp (the bulb exploding),
bureau drawers that had held socks
or sleeping infants, real cribs
and bunk beds,

people completely emptying out,
whole lives flaming like that,
all their belongings, not just bric-a-brac.

What were they thinking?
That it was all junk anyway,
so why not

put the damn stuff out in the alleys,
on the sidewalks and in the gutters, lives
pressed between shoe and arms factories,
the wire and textile mills

on Beacon, Grand, Crystal, and Castle
and on all the streets around

there were fires that drew a crowd,
once ignited, kept burning,
matches set to the towers of troubles
doused with kerosene again and again,
the fire department on a fool's errand:

it was Independence Day.

Escapes

1. We Swim

The ocean seemed unexpectedly rude
when we'd been trying so
hard to avoid an icy encounter.

At the beginning of that one week
every year, our parents upholding
a splash of their vacation truce,

my sisters and I raced away,
leaving behind a path of sandy anger;
released to roam the beach

we flew across the firm strand
to where it was muddy,
having forgotten where we were

— up North, in Maine — so we froze,
halting at the shoreline,
only dipping toes in.

Yet somehow we were able
eventually to tolerate the cold.
And how I remember the pleasure,

that wash of numbness delivered
all afternoon in sea foam, in yards
of kelp twists and slimy, curling weeds

which we believed, made each of us
a goddess who was born to wear
the banner of a new world across her heart.

We buried our feet in the mud,
picked up the unbroken shells
the tide tossed at us,
followed the roads snails made.

We dove into the drink then,
not one of us a real swimmer,

riding waves all afternoon,
floating gently over each shimmering
swell just before breaking,

surrendering to the easy rocking water,
to that deceitful blue heaven,
ignoring the calls of anyone on shore
who warned that we were out too far.

2. Mother Reads the Newspaper

Alone, off for a drive,
leaving us at the cottage
wondering with Father
and muffins and jam,
her route toward Scarborough,
to Cape Elizabeth, cruising
Black Point Road, gone
just to hear herself think.

The car parked facing Higgins Beach,
windows down, soothed by the rush,
the waves breaking, only half hearing
how smooth stones rattle
whenever the tide recedes.

She read the morning paper,
front to back, then returned
just as we began to worry. But
too soon we forgot we'd missed her.

I'll leave you. I'll leave
the whole damn bunch of you,
she threatened when we misbehaved.

We three girls went outside
to sit in the shadows of tall trees,
on Ivy Avenue made a bed of pine needles,
in the salt air breathed deep, singing rounds.

Back home in the city she took us with her
for rides up Sky Drive to the airport,
let us out to play at the runway fence.

Soon we tired of watching piper cubs glide in,
take off, and when she wasn't looking,
focused again on her newspaper spread
like a sun shade across the windshield,
we took off.

She didn't know where we were
and we were happy, reaching our arms up
into the womb of the snack machine
in the terminal lobby, pressing a lever
we figured out how to make popcorn
rain into little paper cups.

3. Sheep Shack

At dawn the sheep put fake noses
up against the window screens
looking into our bedroom.

I don't know what they want.
I do know that I am awake,
that this is no dream,

not the vacation I planned,
falling for the idyllic narrative,
the enticing cove, pinpoint on the map.

It's not just their gaze,
but their odd odor, too, fills the house,
sickens my stomach, so at night I rest
my head on a pillow of pine needles.

It's a backwater, where an old woman
loved her sheep, the ones of the flock
who couldn't make it through winter
where she was raised,
the lighthouse keeper's daughter.

I picture her motor-boating
back home to that island,
her road, the necessary sea,
her life with these animals.

I picture her herding some
into a vulnerable boat,
driving them back to the dock,
the ones who wouldn't survive
in rough elements for long,
like me in this house.

The wind at night makes whatever is upstairs
rattle around like my worries wanting resolution.

One small black and white framed
photo on the wall next to the bed,
a scruffy ewe named Sassafras.

Maybe that one was the first
who wouldn't nurse,
refused to give up its wool
for someone's blanket,
insisted on coming home
to stay with her.

The neighbor who inherited the place
offers no explanation
for how she could advertise
a subsistence life,
as if it were a tourist destination.

TWO

"A conversation is a journey, and what gives it value is fear."

Anne Carson

Dialogues with Mum

1. Sunday Drive to Visit Mum

Past heron nests, the crazy straw baskets,
long necks and beaks jutting out,
silhouetted against the white sky,
odd how they keep their balance
and crown the dead swamp trees.

I know I'm almost there this wintry day
when Wachusett's peak appears on the horizon,
headed to the mountain, seen from the same
stretch of highway where sun illuminates
the stand of silver birch, a single row
at roadside, frail as my mother.

2. I Bring

Steam and flame are the same
to Mother now. The humidifier
next to her bed becomes a *candle*.
She asks that I fill it with water.

When she calls the family dog
she leaves the letter *y*
off her name *Harmony*.
Can she remember how difficult it was
for everyone to get along?

I have tried not to mention accidents
and deaths she doesn't remember,
tried not to correct her when she thinks
I am an aunt she loved,
one gone before my birth.

I bring bottles of spring water:
perhaps she'll remember to drink.

I bring her lacey-top nylon stockings,
charcoal, nude, coal,
the colors she prefers.

On May Day her gift, tiny but gold,
the Blessed Mother medal —
it's her day, too — on a short ribbon
that's heavenly blue.

She remembers the gift of other years,
no longer left on the doorstep
with the morning paper and a row
of empty milk bottles, a note rolled up in one:

she remembers her happiness, finding it
— I wish it could be arranged —
in a straw basket of May flowers
banked with excelsior, spring green.

3. Dressing Room

Last year's clothes unpacked,
no longer suitable, yet perfectly fine
for some other body, better
for my thinner sister maybe.

Mother and her bedroom transformed:
we're in the dressing room at Saks
or Macy's and it's for her to decide
who looks good in what and call the sale.

"Oh, get that! It looks great on you."
Excited as a young girl,
younger even than her daughters,
she wants to try something on,
to be beautiful once again.

Turning right
turning left
at the mirror admiring the fit,
the sweater soft and cheery pink.
"Perfect."

4. The Cure

for Meaghan and Jules

She has a sudden renewed interest in life,
lets the grandchildren paint her fingernails
and her toenails, the color *Tutti Fruiti Tonga,*
yet I never remember her wearing nail polish.

The little one posts on Facebook
a photo of her reading the newspaper,
when I thought she'd given it up.

Her big sister makes a video interview,
asking Mum random questions, then
puts it on YouTube.

She's game for going to the movies
and expects me to take her to the school play.
"Of course I'm going," she says.

She no longer reads the list of forbidden
foods, takes her hearing aid out
to avoid criticism or arguments.

5. Getting Out to See the Moon

Tonight the moon is full, and again
she surprises knowing
the Hunter's Moon comes after
the one that lights the way for harvest.

"We were just driving along and there
it was, suddenly rising out of the mountain."

The trees had lost their leaves.

"It was stuck in the branches.
I've never seen it so big!"

Sometimes things work out better
after plans change,
my visit delaying her ride
in the country with my brother;
so she didn't miss the moon tonight,
wasn't home before sunset.

Wachusett just down the road,
I take her there, too,
for drives on the car road
to the top for the view:
against changing leaves, the reservoir
thick dark blue, like enamel paint
on an old Ford pickup truck.

She recites Algonquin names:
Wolf, Snow, and Worm,
the moons of winter, but then
forgets the rest and I take over
the list someone taught me as a child.

I want to help her remember
the moons of Spring:
Pink, Flower, Strawberry;

and not to forget either
early summer's Buck and Hay moons
and later, the Sturgeon.

She says:
"After this one, two more in fall,
the Beaver and the Cold moon,"
before winter establishes itself.

6. Receiving Guests

She remembers when
my brother saw a crow
perched on the metal
frame of his hospital bed,
his brain inflamed, making him talk
through his hat about phantoms;

but it's her brain all fired up now:
she thinks she has visitors — my sister —
perched at the foot of *her* bed,
my brother and his wife
waiting in the living room,
sitting in the antique wing chairs.

She must throw off her silk comforter,
what she has always called her *puff,*
get up, get dressed or else
they'll think her rude or worse
worry there's something gone wrong
that she's taken to bed
in what she thinks is daylight.

When the word *hardware* comes to her
she remembers where clothes are kept,
knows the ornate brass drawer pulls
will be cold to the touch:
but she must make herself presentable,

tug and pull to get into the mahogany bureau,
rummage around in lingerie, choosing
a flimsy faded pink camisole — no bra —
she isn't going out today — some silk
fancy pants trimmed in Raschel lace.

But the armoire choices prove most baffling:
blouses, sweaters, no slacks — she never wore
slacks — but there are dresses in six sizes.

A mad shopper lost in the racks,
trying to find just the right skirt to *Wow*,
the wire hangers putting up a good fight,
intertwined on the pole. *Now where is that*
Nile green gown, the one she wore
just once in the forties to a dance?

Struggling for balance she manages
to dress herself, pulls through
her wispy fine white hair
the familiar soft bristle brush
she used grooming all four babies.

Ready, down the corridor she goes,
expecting to find her visitors waiting,

but her roomy house is eerie,
just full of night missing its moon, and
she is alone, the clock ticking away
on the Governor Winthrop desk,
time illuminated in a dark corner
of the next room.

7. Selling Her Car

"How old is that car?" I asked.
          "1942," she said.

"1942? This is the 21st century, Mum."
          "Right. I bought that car in 1942,
          paid it off the year before your father
          died. He said he wanted to pay it off
          and I said, *what if we need the money
          for a nursing home?* He said, *Like hell!*"

"Mum, he died in 1993."
          "1993?"

"Yes, 1993."
          "I paid off the car the year before, 1992."

"That's right. 1992, not 1942."
          "Oh, I don't know. I'm going backwards.
          Pretty soon I'll be in 1620."

8. Gianni Plays for Mum

You play Glazounov's *Quartet, opus 109*:
"Canzona variée," which you are preparing
for a recital. I hold out the phone
for Mum to hear. She's miles away,
doesn't know it.

"He's got good timing," she says.

Other calls, she remarked on his tone,
but time is on her mind these days.

"And doesn't the other one play
an instrument, too?" she asks.
"What other one?" I say.

"The girl – what instrument does she play?"
What girl? My daughter?"
"Yes, that one."

I tell her I don't have a daughter.
"Oh, you don't? Now why did I think that?
Who was I thinking of? A cousin maybe?"

I thank my son for leaving his door open
so she could hear him practice.
"You know," I say, "she loves
hearing you play, and she misses you."

In truth I'm not sure
she knows who he is either.

It pleased her though that he played and promised
to visit soon, bring his horn next time to serenade her
with Gershwin or Weill, and she'd love it if
he'd learn, "What a Wonderful World."

9. Doubt

Some days she lives
in neighborhoods where
she can't get lost:

at the corner house
she finds her aunt and cousins,

then at *Fine Point* —
No, (she makes the correction),
Pine Point,
all her summer friends live
on a mound of sand
(she means the beachfront).

And off the country road
there is what she calls
the homestead. She'd been there
visiting she thought, out all day,
enjoying *spring,* the wrong season.
She says the trees along the way were
a full-leafed canopy to pass under.

Sometimes though, a question
escapes when she opens
the refrigerator, empty
of everything but doubt,

or when she surveys faces
in the living room — someone
in the wing chair — and who
are those two on the couch?

Where is everyone,
the people she knew
when she couldn't get lost?

In nine decades she has found
her way to lost, says, *I*
haven't seen my mother
or my father in so long.
I don't know why,
don't know what's going on.

When I call to say I'll visit
she says: *Do you know*
where I am now?
I'm not in the old place.

It isn't spring at all
when this is happening —
the harvest is already in —
the flower shops have
chrysanthemum. The temperature
dips lower overnight.
Wheels of Queen Anne's Lace
dry up, turn inward
into tight brown nests.

THREE

"Of course we must die.
How else will the world be rid of
the old telephone numbers
we cannot forget?"

Charles Reznikoff

The Sadness

I didn't know why and
I didn't know what to do.

She was

having a good cry for herself
on the morning rush hour train,
a young girl, a teenager,
only about as old as my son.

I could see she was not dressed
warmly enough for such a cold day;
though she had the sense
to dress in layers,
she was all in cotton:
thin jacket over a blouse,
summer weight slacks,
no hat, no gloves, no scarf.

Standing at the jolt for my stop
I crossed the aisle, took her hand,
unfolded it. I could offer nothing
but a tissue, one I found
in my pocket. Clean but crumpled.

"Thank you. Thank you," she said.

Observing the Orchestra Rehearsal

"So close, so tense, so rich.
Compare this with anything
you ever did in your life,
with the Paganini we did last week,
with any of Bach.

"What would you say about the beginning?
Does it give life?
Is it beneath the dark earth? Above the earth?
Is it happy music?
No! No!
It's coming from underneath the murky water."

The straw-haired girl says she has mixed feelings.

And Charlie waves his hand so beautifully.
He says, *The music is anxious.*

"So then,
no *Twinkle, Twinkle, Little Star*, huh?"

Small Town: A Death

The commuter train this morning
on the tracks that run behind the school
blows its whistle as it passes by, for the girl
who was killed the afternoon before,
crossing over, taking a short cut home,
a hole in the fence patched up from time to time.

The train sounds its whistle, too, for the others
who'll repeat her action, the whistle to warn them:
Careful, it's coming.

Last night taking a wrong turn somehow
I came upon her street, the neighborhood
of small and simple ranch houses, the one
in the dark unmistakable and not
for the funeral drape above the door
or a huddle of neighbors bearing
casseroles, flowering plants, cakes.

I remembered when my father died
a friend carrying on the custom of bringing
something living and something sweet,
left on the porch a feathery fern
and a jar of lavender honey.

But at the girl's house, a police car was posted,
out front the vans with wired poles and lights;
reporters, photographers parked their cars
a few houses down, while others searching
for a story gathered around the corner.

How cruel the piled up fallen leaves
coloring the driveway, blanketing the front lawn.

Shrine in Cambridge

In this city of scholars and artists
here is where one young friend shot another
by accident. In this place, faithfully tended:
a cauldron of sentiment. I see a man or
sometimes a woman, planting a reflection
of whatever the season or holiday. Notice
in autumn some yellow and rusty chrysanthemum.
Then a small evergreen tree or holly and berries
strung with garlands of battery-operated lights.

At the first of the year, a miniature rose
in the clay pot and a champagne bottle beside it.
I can't tell as I drive by if it's been uncorked.

The occasions keep coming:
every year a birthday cake and candles
and a balloon on a wooden wand, stuck in the soil
with whatever is left from Valentine's Day.
Yet no one makes wishes, and no one is served.

I used to walk past the place, so I know
friends of the boys come, carve messages
with knives all along the aluminum railing
at the nearby footbridge. I remember one:
Seanie Pooh — Hollah Back, it said.

What on earth were they doing with the gun?
They were friends and it was an accident.
That's what everyone heard. They were coming
up out of the woods surrounding the reservoir,
had been walking along the railroad tracks.

They'd been below the avenue
of million dollar houses, just down the street
from the soccer field. It was Friday night

so there were no games for the children's league,
the teams not named for pirates, patriots, pioneers,
or guardians — but for colors like
teal, ivory, fuchsia, and lime.

In this city of scholars and artists one friend
shot the other by accident, and the one who did
dragged his friend's body and his grief
up the hill, under the hemlocks and pine,
to the sidewalk, and he held him in lap
and they were a Pieta while evening
rush hour passed them by. One friend kneeled
over the other, wailing,
showing what he'd done,
while the other bled into the traffic jam.

Red Things

Underground waiting for the next train,
I'm looking years later across the tracks
where there are red things for sale:
Red Sox baseball caps, a pyramid of
stuffed bears with hearts on the outside,
scarves and mufflers, even a silk negligee
fitted on a headless mannequin;

and then I remember the month and day.

In the hospital room it was also February,
a Valentines Day snow out the window,
the world moving into slush and mud.

There was an extra day in the month,
a liberty taken by a printer, a mistake
in the record of days remaining for my friend,
the calendar picture of a sunset on the wall,
lying fiery numbers not showing
what the visitors knew,
that it was the wrong year for leaping.

The technician's cart sporting a rose in a vase
pushed its way through the channel
where you were swimming. He'd come
to take blood, though it was pointless.

When the not-so-alluring voice
came over the intercom
you spoke of hammers,
the static, a banging noise.

The dinner tray delivered
a full glass of cranberry juice
and a painted heart cookie.

Name, Address, Phone Number Drawer

Last night going through
a drawer full of corners
torn from envelopes of old
birthday cards and letters,
written on them and on
grocery slips, phone numbers too,
not just the names of streets
where the now-dead used to live.

In a cabinet meant for good china, linens,
shelves of crystal glassware, in the room
where we still sit for the old-fashioned
evening meal, I'm clinging to those long gone.

I imagine them in ghost paradise, strolling,
watching me sifting through the pieces,
fretting I won't weed their scraps of paper,
hating that I continue this sort of life list,
as if I'm some birder, keeping
a record of all my sightings.

I may never sort out what's in this drawer
along with the self-extinguishing candles,
the plug to recharge the phone,
the "double-life" replacement bulbs for the lamp.

I choose to let it be, my way of remembering,
a house and a street lined with trees
or the apartment building in a tough neighborhood,
and the voice I would hear on the other
end of the line. I keep refusing
to discount numbers now owned by others,
the houses full of people I don't know.

FOUR

"Love and scandal are the best sweeteners of tea."

Henry Fielding

Lines Inspired by a Horse

A horse trotting to the fence
knows in one lick it's fallen
for the trick of one who comes
empty handed, only wanting kisses.
Tongue rolling, unrolling,
searching for the missing sugar-apple-carrot,
deprived even of a stroke of the mane,
just left to scrounge white clover, to pose
in the middle of the field for passersby.

When I return you will not know me
or you will pretend to be blind and deaf
or occupied with the breeze ruffling and fraying
what remains of leaves on the Osage orange,
the rain blasting trumpets of morning glory,
shaking trees so you will remember the clunk
of walnuts falling to the ground.

When you see me again you will seem
so deep in contemplation of stone or mud
that you will not even notice me.
You may pretend or really be sleeping in that way
that seems not like rest for having to keep on
holding yourself up, though your head bows
and your body twitches.

I admit I walked away with sadness
when I had nothing to give, seeing
flies glued like freckles across your nostrils.
I walked away not knowing the payment
exacted, not expecting the disappearing act,
how the gentlest tug can remove an outer layer,
sneak up on you when you least expect it,
how any creature will take
the scent of your clothing as a substitute for you.

Shop of Small Pleasures

Inside there is a room
beyond the velvet blue drape
and the window lure, the cape
sparkling from rhinestones pinned to it,
and ruffles and promises:
the suite of the carefully arranged.

No costume tiaras or anything
precious, but some humming
and next to the locket missing a picture,
a pair of shoes with thin, high heels,
shoes that walk, not run away.

While an old radio was playing on a shelf,
dirty plastic pretend ivory thing,
voice on the smooth side,

I held you one last time and you
wanted to know what it felt like.
"Like Christmas," I said,
though I knew you'd given me
just a gift-boxed souvenir.

Soap Opera

The hasty dinner and running out after
to the music hall, late for the concert.

Home to dishes left in the sink.

The women of the orchestra
had such presence, and they come
into the kitchen, too, and the wife

considers them while soaping the glasses,
their long dresses of silk velvet
and such interesting shoes.

The attic vent opens and closes.

"You need work," the husband says.
"Money would be good."

There's wind tonight, the wife thinks.

Then the clink of forks and knives
in the stainless steel sink.

Kitten, spike, wedge heels
of the women's shoes, their feet
stayed still in them
while they plucked the strings.

The wind was singing at the birdfeeder.
The house, not warm enough this winter,
the apartment below vacant,
the floorboards cold.

The women's cheeks glowed in crescendo
more rosy as the weight of the music
accumulated.

Lover Boy Fiction

One summer he taught me how to take
corn from a neighbor's field
to feed his chickens. I'd be lost in thought
by the time I reached the corner fence post.

An ear of corn was nothing to him.
He stole his own car,
set it on fire, collected the insurance.

I fell in love with the sun as much as with him,
the sun at the end of an afternoon,
when it lit up the silken tufts, warmed
the towering green stalks — so beautiful
as I snapped their yield —
there in the corn rows, hidden from view.

As I lay with him in the house beyond, I could hear
fallen limbs hung on sturdier branches.
They kept moving back and forth, creaking,
creaking in the wind, keeping time
as I filled up my arms.

Ecstasy

On the bureau we found the silver jewelry,
the ring, bangle, hoop,
in a puddle of wax already starting to set,

still hot to our fingertips,
the candle burned down to its wick
while we'd been swinging on stars.

We were astounded:
we might have burned alive.

FIVE

"It was like being born again. The colors were different, the feeling of things you had right down inside yourself was different..."

from *Voyage in the Dark*
Jean Rhys, born 1890,
in Roseau, Dominica

The Landing (Commonwealth of Dominica)

In the little plane of prayers
we look out little windows

watch the mountainside
as it grows, as the pilot
rubs our noses in it,
in the terrifying
angle of our course.

We drift: first look,
a calculation and then
the pilot gunning for a landing,
quick descent, seizing opportunity:
he knows there is only one
and all of us on the little plane of prayers
hope he's found it.

The boy in the next seat
asks for his future:
"Do you think there is
a flat place to land?"

We hear progeny, old age,
the longing of the ages
in that logical question.

No one answers:
we can only pray to ourselves.

As the little plane moves away from
a placid sea below, we keep silence,
the earth shown to us as if
through a magnifying glass, grotesque
because we are too close.

We do bump down, our *yes*
settling in a dust cloud, dirt
landing strip appearing out of nowhere,
blessing our magician/pilot/guide.

It's a cow path really that we travel,
becoming after a while, tarmac.
We breathe with the terminal in view,
Melville Hall, shack of a wayfarer's station,
the journey beginning again.

Guide to Soufriere

The path you take
leads up the hill above the beach,
cuts right between the two seas:

the Atlantic will look
rough and cold, and this
is where you come from;

the Caribbean is not grey
but blue, like a swimming pool,
and it will invite you in.

In lush Soufricrc
a man on the beach
in a fruit tree
with his machete
is not a criminal.

You can take a handful
of coral like chalk
but won't need
to write anything
on a dark, flat stone.

Colored boats drift
like crayons or fingers
splayed, showing
a perfect hand.

You will see as you come and go
the card players at roadside
in front of small tin shacks
listing from rain or wind,
the weight of everything
in the blistering sun,
have nothing to lose.

And a woman in a long skirt
will walk barefoot down the road,
jug of something on her head,
elegantly stubborn in Paradise,
sweeping her body
down a dusty way.

Sorcery

On this island hummingbirds drink
from blue banana flowers, and orchids
in the cloud forest attach themselves
to every tree, making you fall for them,

leading to confusion and forgetting
who you are you begin to think:
am I a flower, a bird,
or maybe I'm a tree?

On this island you will find
The Valley of Desolation and also
the sometimes dried up Boiling Lake.

You will hear, too, the dove,
it's awful sad cry, because
in the rainforest even the sadness
of a dove has more muscle.

And the pigeon with a red neck coos,
comforting the trembler,
and the pearly-eyed thrasher.

Solitaire

Don't go looking for that bird.
Don't let yourself be fooled.

Remember the local legend
about the solitaire's song,
two long notes, as if somewhere
a gate is squeaking to let you in.

Careful:

it is wanting
not the oil of silence, but rather
to be heard over great distances,

to reach into a soul, the way
a saxophone does, alluring
in its spell of *let's get lost.*

Ascent

I, too, have known the long walk,
without a car would forgo
the bus ride, not suited
to waiting in depot or doorway,
patience skittish around me.

On the road to Trois Piton:
those with work in Roseau
and schoolchildren head home.

Let out for the day, some stand
waiting for the bus, some walk

In the snackette in town, Psalm 21
written in cursive on one wall
painted institution green, the mural,
the mountains looming,
background for the song

that I would sing this way:

Let me keep in sight where I have to go;
hold firm my footing, even in the rain;
let me not slip; let me tolerate blinding sun
and nights when there is no moon.

Mountain Road from Roseau

Our cares lifting out to sea
all afternoon, lulled by the scent
of what was on the breeze:
was it frangipani, oleander

that made us forget the way home
would be reduced to barely,
where the mountain blocks one lane?

Riding switchbacks, blinding glitter,
sun hitting *what?* we hear rattling
as the van leans into the bend.

I want our driver
to blow the horn,
to genuflect *please.*

It's a day when the market is closed,
yet farm trucks don't stay idle,
although empty of the usual
citrus, coconuts, chickens;
packed instead with tourists
off the ship we saw
docked in Port at Roseau.

We swallow hard hearing
cries of merriment and terror
as the vehicle comes hard
down the mountain.

I pray our driver will remember
his own youth and the schoolgirls,
the ones we saw hiding grey uniforms
under red umbrellas, silk torches of love
and all their desires, skipping down the alleys,
staying too long downtown, missing their bus
and walking now this same shoulder less road.

In the van's front seat my son Gianni
rides shotgun, holds his breath,
pretending to be brave.

We are all afraid
I want to tell him,
even the driver who refuses to bow
to the sharp cliff dropping off one side,
to the stone on the other, jutting
into narrow corridors of the heart.

Generosity (a short litany before sleep)
for Rachel and Curtis

Praise
the downtown street

Praise
all the buses departing Roseau
which have names not numbers

Praise
Sweety's, God's in Control,
Too Much to Mention, Not Mine,
General Love and *Parce Que* —
my favorite — the *Because* Bus

Praise
for Carmen Watt
and her *Licensed Tavern,*
the menu on a hand-painted board

Praise the blood of island fruit and herbs:
juice made of sorrel, sour sop, cherry,
barbadine, grapefruit, carambola,
pineapple, orange, passion fruit, guava

Praise
the light breeze that sweeps
the coconut palm fronds

Praise
the rain coming down heavier,
dousing the smoky fires

Praise
that Someone who is humming

Praise then the whole forest, humming, too.

ABOUT THE AUTHOR

Mary Bonina's poetry, fiction and memoir has appeared in *Salamander, Hanging Loose, Gulf Stream*, in many other journals and several anthologies, including *Voices of the City*, from Rutgers University Center for Ethnicity, Culture, and Modern Experience and Hanging Loose Press (2004). She is the author of *Lunch in Chinatown* and the chapbook *Living Proof* (Červená Barva Press, 2007). An excerpt from her memoir *My Father's Eyes* received Honorable Mention in the University of New Orleans Study Abroad Competition (2009). As winner of Boston Contemporary Authors, a public art project, her poem "Drift" was etched in a granite monolith permanently installed outside a busy Boston subway station in Jamaica Plain. Bonina is a fellow of the Virginia Center for the Creative Arts and has also been awarded a fellowship by the Vermont Studio Center. Her photographs of mid-coast Maine are included in *Camden, Maine: Belfast to Port Clyde, a Photographic Portrait* (Twin Lights Publishers, 2001). Bonina holds an MFA from the Program for Writers at Warren Wilson College.